Mountains

by Jeffery L. Williams

Published in the United States of America
by the Hameray Publishing Group, Inc.

Copyright © 2016 Hameray Publishing Group, Inc.

Publisher: Raymond Yuen
Editor: Tara Rodriquez
Editorial Assistant: Shana Baldassari
Cover Designer: Anita Adams
Book Designer: Stephani Rosenstein

Photo Credits: Page i – Vaclav Volrab; Page 2 – Samuel Borges Photography (child), Bon Appetit (mountain); Page 3 – Volodymyr Burdiak; Page 4 – George W. Bailey (heat), Daulon (pressure); Page 5 – Andrea Danti; Page 6 – Andrea Danti; Page 7 – Vadim Sadovski (planet), Justin Reznick (inset); Page 8 – Alex GK Lee; Page 9 – Ammit Jack; Page 10 – Robert Crow; Page 11 – Vadim Petrakov; Page 12 – Stefansonn; Page 13 – Kucher Serhii; Page 14 – Olga Kovalenko (pencil), Corbac40 (mountain); Page 15 – NancyS

All rights reserved. No part of this publication may be reproduced or transmitted in any form or by any means without permission in writing from the publisher. Reproduction of any part of this book, through photocopy, recording, or any electronic or mechanical retrieval system without the written permission of the publisher, is an infringement of the copyright law.

ISBN 978-1-62817-571-4

Printed in Singapore

1 2 3 4 5 6 7 IPS 22 21 20 19 18 17 16

Table of Contents

Heat.. 6

The force of pressure.................. 12

Mountain facts 16

Glossary 17

Index 18

Do you know how a mountain is made?

All mountains start as flat land. Some mountains were made a long time ago, and some mountains are still being made today.

One way a mountain is made is by heat. Another way a mountain is made is from **pressure**.

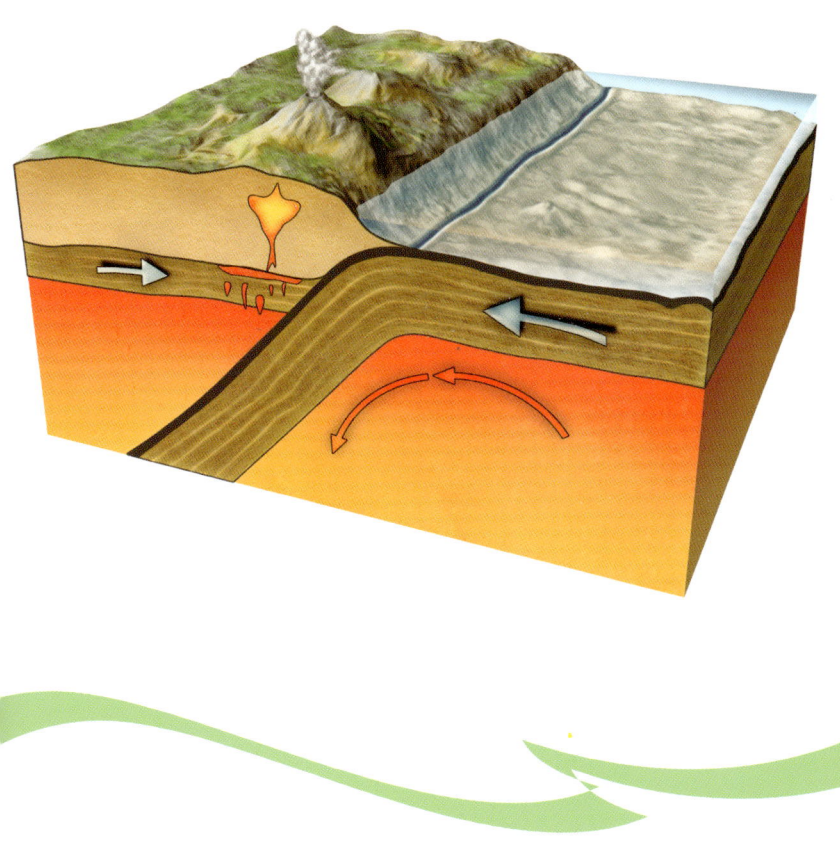

All mountains are made by heat or pressure or both!

Heat

One way a mountain is made is with heat.

Inside the earth, it is hot enough to melt rock!

Sometimes this hot melted rock, or **magma**, boils up through the earth's **crust**.

A **volcano** is a mountain that is made this way.

The magma comes up through the crust. Then it cools off and turns back into rock.

As more and more magma boils up and cools off, it adds layers to the mountain, and the mountain gets bigger and bigger.

The Force of Pressure
Another way a mountain is made is with pressure. Pressure is a force that causes things to move.

When you put a little pressure on your pencil lead, it will move and cause a black line. The earth's crust is always moving from a little pressure.

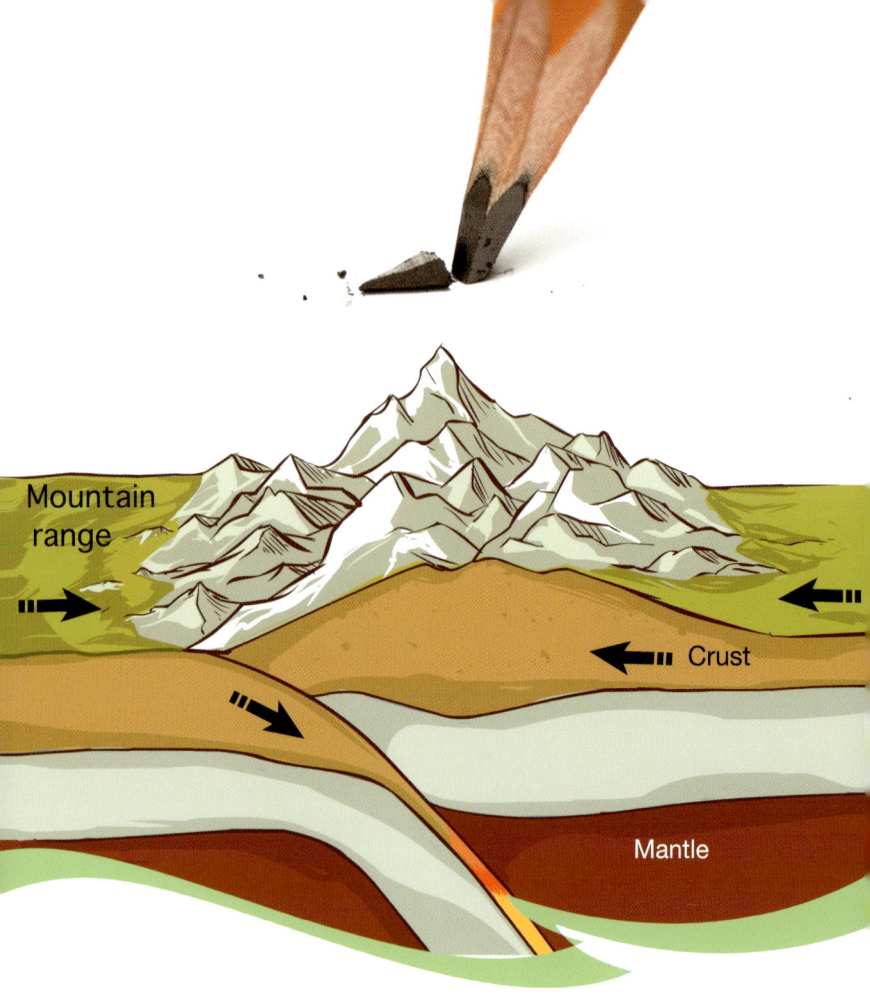

But if you put too much pressure on a pencil, the lead will break. And when too much pressure builds up under the earth's crust, it pushes up very hard and breaks the crust.

Rocks pushed up from the crust become mountains.

Mountain Facts

- There are mountains all over the earth.
- A line of mountains is called a mountain range.
- Most mountains are millions of years old.
- Wind and water can make a mountain get smaller.
- There are mountains on the moon and on other planets.
- All mountains on every planet are made from heat or pressure.
- Mount Everest is the tallest mountain in the world.
- Mount Denali is the tallest mountain in the United States.
- The Winter Olympics have to be held near mountains for skiing sports.

Glossary

crust: the top layer of the earth, which is made of solid rocks

force: a push or a pull

magma: lava; melted rock

pressure: a force that pushes on something

volcano: a mountain that has an opening in the earth's crust where magma comes out

Index

crust, 8, 10, 13–15
heat, 5–11
magma, 8, 10–11
pressure, 5, 12–15
volcano, 9